Tuscan Cookbook

Tuscan Recipes for True Tuscan Italian Cooking

By
BookSumo Press
All rights reserved

Published by
http://www.booksumo.com

ENJOY THE RECIPES?

KEEP ON COOKING WITH 6 MORE FREE COOKBOOKS!

Visit our website and simply enter your email address to join the club and receive your 6 cookbooks.

http://booksumo.com/magnet

https://www.instagram.com/booksumopress/

https://www.facebook.com/booksumo/

LEGAL NOTES

All Rights Reserved. No Part Of This Book May Be Reproduced Or Transmitted In Any Form Or By Any Means. Photocopying, Posting Online, And / Or Digital Copying Is Strictly Prohibited Unless Written Permission Is Granted By The Book's Publishing Company. Limited Use Of The Book's Text Is Permitted For Use In Reviews Written For The Public.

Table of Contents

Tuscano Mussels with Linguini 7

Chicken Kale Skillet 8

Homey Potato Casserole 9

Crimini Pasta Bake 10

White Wine Chicken Stew 11

Romano Rigatoni Casserole 12

Asiago Tuna Spread 13

Lemon Steak with Parmesan Salad 14

Cheesy Chicken Cream Pasta 15

Chunky Spinach Bean Soup 16

Famous Zuppa Toscana 17

Mustard Sausage Soup 18

Sunny Hot Spaghetti 19

Cannellini Sausage Pie 20

Zesty Chicken Roast 21

Traditional Italian Mussels 22

Parmesan Beef Cakes 23

Nutty Vanilla Biscuits 24

Tomato Cream Dip 25

Saucy Beef Skillet 26

Sunny Ranch Chicken Soup 27

Milanese Torta 28

Puttanesca 29

Italian Style Cod 30

Clams Toscano 31

Pasta Rustic 32

Simple Sundried Tomato Pasta 33

Pepperoni Pasta 34

A Light Thai Inspired Pasta 35

Bacon Linguine 36

Easy Mushroom Pasta 37

Cajun Style Penne 38

Fresh Seasoning Pasta 39

Alfredo Done Right 40

Pasta Cajun II 41

Clams, Shrimp, and Snapper Stew 42

Meatballs Done Right 43

Easy Biscotti 44

Italian Tuscan Soup 45

Chicken Marsala Classico 46

Maggie's Easy Bruschetta 47

Authentic Eggplant Parmesan 48

Roman Fun Pasta 49

Zucchini and Spinach Soup 50

Classical Risotto 51

Tortellini Classico 52

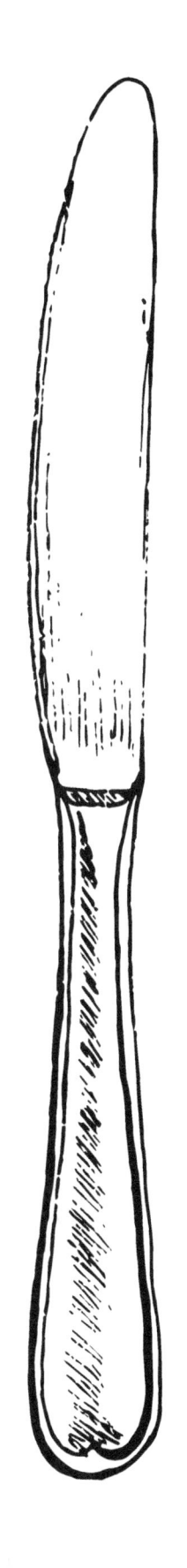

Feta Fettucine 53

Authentic Meatball Sub 54

Capers and Tilapia 55

Southern Italian Chicken 56

Roast Beef Sandwiches 57

Tortellini 58

Italian Baked Turkey-Loaf 59

Restaurant Style Primavera 60

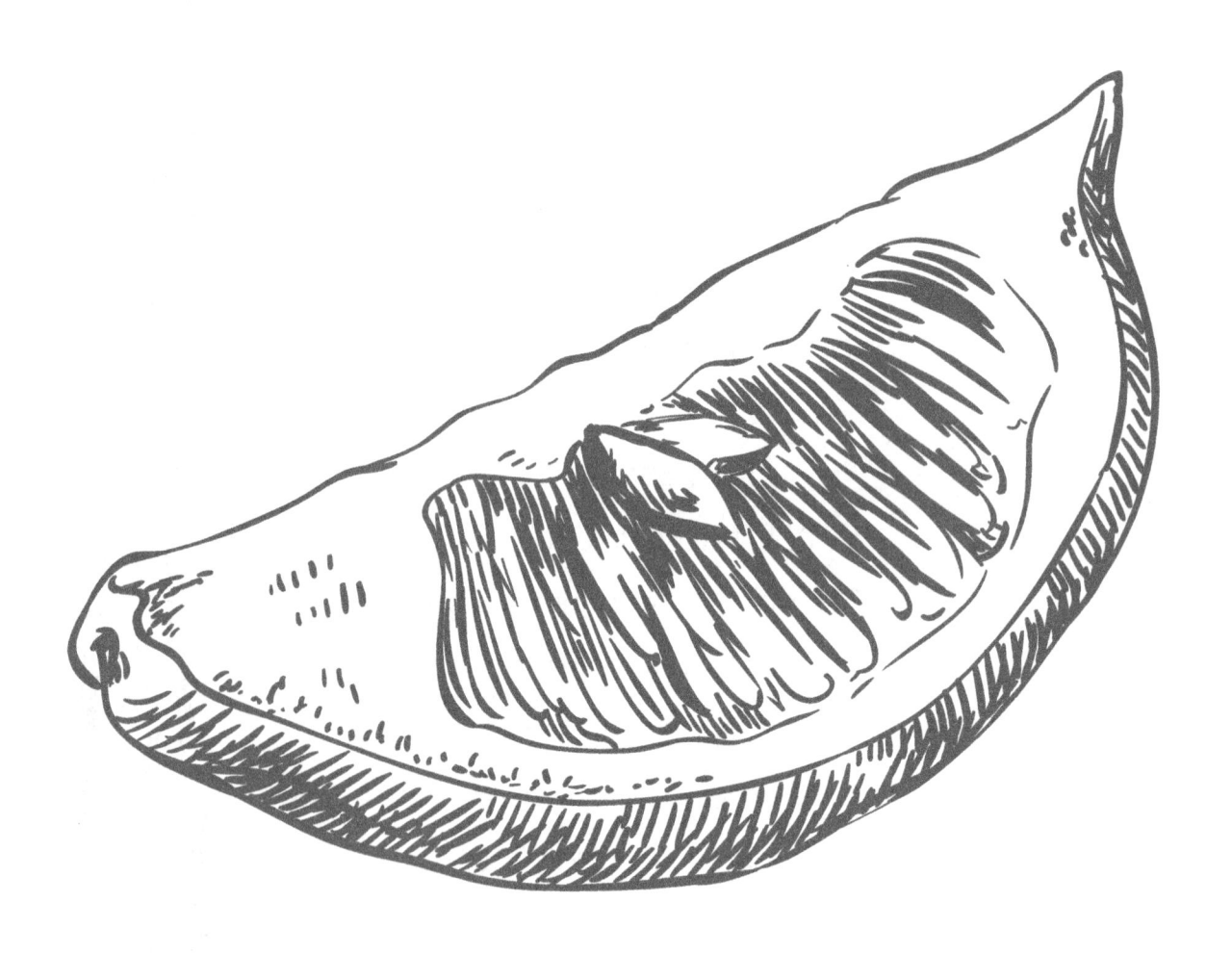

Tuscano Mussels with Linguini

Prep Time: 5 mins
Total Time: 20 mins

Servings per Recipe: 4
Calories   304 kcal
Fat   5.4 g
Carbohydrates   52.8g
Protein   13 g
Cholesterol   9 mg
Sodium   188 mg

Ingredients

1 tbsp olive oil
1 clove garlic, minced
1 (14.5 oz.) can crushed tomatoes
1/2 tsp dried oregano
1/2 tsp dried basil
1 pinch crushed red pepper flakes

1/4 C. white wine
1 lb. mussels, cleaned and debearded
8 oz. linguini pasta
1 lemon - cut into wedges, for garnish

Directions

1. In a pan of lightly salted boiling water, cook the pasta for about 8-10 minutes and drain well.
2. Meanwhile in a large pan, heat the oil on medium heat and sauté the garlic till tender.
3. Stir in the tomatoes, herbs and red pepper flakes and reduce the heat to low.
4. Simmer for about 5 minutes.
5. Add the mussels and wine and increase the heat to high.
6. Cook for about 3-5 minutes.
7. Place the mussels mixture over pasta and drizzle with the lemon juice.
8. Serve with a garnishing of the parsley and lemon wedges.

CHICKEN
Kale Skillet

Prep Time: 10 mins
Total Time: 30 mins

Servings per Recipe: 4
Calories	355 kcal
Fat	10.1 g
Cholesterol	19.3g
Sodium	28.9 g
Carbohydrates	59 mg
Protein	164 mg

Ingredients

1 lb boneless, skinless chicken breasts, sliced
2 tbsps I Can't Believe It's Not Butter!(R) Spread, divided
4 C. LIGHTLY packed chopped kale leaves
2 cloves garlic, finely chopped
1 package Knorr(R) Rice Sides(TM) - Cheddar Broccoli
1/4 C. sun-dried tomatoes, thinly sliced
Lemon wedges

Directions

1. Place a large skillet on medium heat. Add to it 1 tbsp of spread and cook it until it melts.
2. Season the chicken with some salt and pepper then cook it in the skillet for 5 min. Drain it and set it aside.
3. Add the remaining spread to the skillet and cook it unit it melts. Add the garlic with kale and cook them for 4 min.
4. Stir in the water and coo them until they start boiling. Add the knorr rice with sun-dried tomatoes and prepare then cook them according the manufacturer's instructions.
5. Add the chicken and combine them completely. Serve your chicken kale skillet warm and enjoy.

Homey Potato Casserole

Prep Time: 15 mins
Total Time: 50 mins

Servings per Recipe: 6
Calories   330.5
Fat   30.7 g
Cholesterol   167.6 mg
Sodium   537.3 mg
Carbohydrates   1.8 g
Protein   11 g

Ingredients

- 1 tbsp salted butter
- 1 red bell pepper
- 1 (24 oz) package Simply Potatoes Homestyle Slices
- 1 (12 oz) package pepper turkey bacon
- 4 eggs

Directions

1. Before you do anything set the oven to 350 F. Grease a large casserole dish with butter or oil.
2. Place a large skillet on medium to high heat. Cook in it the bacon until it becomes crisp. Drain it and place it on some paper towels to drain then crumble it.
3. Cut the bell peppers into strips. Place a large skillet on medium to high heat. Cook in it 1/2 tbsp of butter until it melts. Add the bell pepper strips and cook them for 5 min.
4. Spread the potato in the bottom of the greased casserole dish. Top it with bacon and bell pepper.
5. Cover the dish with a piece of foil then cook it in the oven for 28 min.
6. Discard the piece of foil and crack the eggs on top of the potato casserole. Place it back in the oven and cook it for 10 min. Serve the potato casserole warm.
7. Enjoy.

CRIMINI
Pasta Bake

 Prep Time: 15 mins
 Total Time: 50 mins

Servings per Recipe: 6
Calories   354.1
Fat   11.4 g
Cholesterol   19.6 mg
Sodium   1593.8 mg
Carbohydrates   48.2 g
Protein   15.6 g

Ingredients

- 8 h crimini mushrooms
- 1 C. broccoli floret
- 1 C. spinach, fresh leaf, tightly packed
- 2 red bell peppers, julienned
- 1 large onion, chopped
- 1 C. mozzarella cheese, shredded
- 1 C. tomato sauce
- 2/3 lb pasta (fettuccine or penne works well)
- 1/3 C. parmesan cheese, grated
- 3 tbsps herbes de provence
- 2 tbsps extra virgin olive oil
- 1 tbsp salt
- 1/2 tbsp pepper

Directions

1. Before you do anything set the oven to 450 F. Grease a casserole dish with oil or cooking spray.
2. Get a large mixing bowl: Toss the mushrooms, broccoli, spinach, pepper, and onion in it. Add 1 tbsp of olive oil, salt, pepper and toss them again.
3. Spread the veggies in the greased dish and cook it in the oven for 10 min.
4. Cook the pasta until it becomes dente. Drain the pasta and set it aside.
5. Get a large mixing bowl: Mix 1 tbsp of olive oil with baked veggies, pasta, herbs and mozzarella cheese. Spread the mix back in the casserole dish.
6. Sprinkle the cheese on top then cook it for 20 min. Serve it warm and enjoy.

White Wine Chicken Stew

Prep Time: 10 mins
Total Time: 50 mins

Servings per Recipe: 4
Calories   299.3
Fat   6.1 g
Cholesterol   68.1 mg
Sodium   390.5 mg
Carbohydrates   30.5 g
Protein   24.3 g

Ingredients

skinless chicken thighs
1 1/2 tsps olive oil
1 yellow onion, thinly sliced
2 red peppers, thinly sliced
2 garlic cloves, minced
1 (28 oz) canpeeled tomatoes
2/3 C. dry white wine
1 tsp dried oregano or 1 large fresh oregano sprig, chopped
1 (14 1/2 oz) can cannellini beans, drained and rinsed
salt and pepper
4 sprigs oregano (optional)

Directions

1. Place a large skillet on medium heat. Heat the oil in it. Add the chicken thighs and cook them for 5 min on each side. Drain them and set them aside.
2. Stir the peppers with onion into the skillet and cook them for 4 min. Stir in the garlic and cook them for 1 min.
3. Reserve the tomato liquid. Mash the tomato until it becomes like a paste. Stir it with the chicken, wine and oregano into the skillet.
4. Cook them until they start simmering then simmer them for 30 min. Stir in the cannellini beans then cook them for another 5 min. Serve your stew warm.
5. Enjoy.

ROMANO Rigatoni Casserole

Prep Time: 30 mins
Total Time: 55 mins

Servings per Recipe: 6
Calories   795.6
Fat   37.6 g
Cholesterol   166.2 mg
Sodium   1842.2 mg
Carbohydrates   73.2 g
Protein   41.2 g

Ingredients

1 lb ground sausage (I use Sage flavor)
1 (28 oz) can Italian-style tomato sauce
1 (14 1/2 oz) can cannellini beans, drained and rinsed
1 (16 oz) BOX rigatoni pasta
1/2 tsp minced garlic
1 tsp italian seasoning
3 C. shredded mozzarella cheese
1/4 C. romano cheese, grated
chopped parsley, to garnish

Directions

1. Before you do anything set the oven to 350 F. Grease a large casserole dish with some butter or oil.
2. Place a large pot on medium heat. Add the garlic with sausages and cook them for 6 min. Add the tomato sauce, beans and Italian seasoning then cook them for 5 min on low heat.
3. Cook the pasta according to the manufacturer's directions. Drain the pasta and sit it into the pot.
4. Pour half of the sausage pasta mix in the greased casserole then top it with half of the mozzarella cheese. Repeat the process to make another layer.
5. Top the casserole with romano cheese then put on it a piece of foil. Cook the rigatoni casserole in the oven for 26 min.
6. Serve your rigatoni warm.
7. Enjoy.

Asiago Tuna Spread

Prep Time: 5 mins
Total Time: 35 mins

Servings per Recipe: 4
Calories   161.8
Fat   3.8 g
Cholesterol   37.5 mg
Sodium   674.6 mg
Carbohydrates   9 g
Protein   23.1 g

Ingredients

2 (6 oz) cans tuna in water, drained
2 shallots, peeled (or one if quite large)
1 (6 1/2 oz) jar artichoke hearts, drained
1/4 C. sun-dried tomato packed in oil, not drained (use 1/4 C. tomatoes and 3 T of the olive oil it comes in, an 8.5 oz jar will make this recipe th)
1/4 C. asiago cheese
1/2 tsp cayenne pepper
1/2 tsp salt
1/2 tbsp dried basil (or more, to taste) or 1/2 tbsp fresh basil (or more, to taste)

Directions

1. Get a food processor: Add all the ingredients and pulse them several time until they become chunky.
2. Get a large mixing bowl: Pour the dip into it then place it in the fridge for 2 h to an 12 h.
3. Serve your dip with some chip, breasdsticks or veggies.
4. Enjoy.

LEMON STEAK with Parmesan Salad

🥣 Prep Time: 10 mins
🕐 Total Time: 20 mins

Servings per Recipe: 4
Calories   265
Fat   24.4 g
Cholesterol   18.7 mg
Sodium   337.7 mg
Carbohydrates   3.3 g
Protein   9.4 g

Ingredients

5 tbsps extra virgin olive oil, plus 1 tsp extra virgin olive oil
1 tbsp fresh-squeezed lemon juice
2 garlic cloves, minced
1 tbsp chopped fresh parsley
1 tbsp chopped fresh oregano
salt
fresh coarse ground black pepper
4 boneless strip steaks, 1 to 1 1/4 inches thick
8 C. loosely packed arugula, washed and dried
3 oz parmesan cheese, cut into thin shavings

Directions

1. To make the dressing:
2. Get a mixing bowl: Whisk the 5 tbsps of olive oil with lemon juice, garlic, parsley, oregano and a pinch each of salt and pepper.
3. Place a large skillet on medium to high heat. Add 1 tsp of oil to it and heat it.
4. Season the steaks strips with some salt and pepper. Cook them in the skillet for 7 min on each side.
5. Lay the arugula leaves in 4 serving plates then top them with the steaks strips, lemon dressing and cheese. Serve your salads right away.
6. Enjoy.

Cheesy Chicken Cream Pasta

Prep Time: 45 mins
Total Time: 1 hr

Servings per Recipe: 6
Calories	1081.4
Fat	48.5 g
Cholesterol	241.6 mg
Sodium	1738.5 mg
Carbohydrates	91.5 g
Protein	66.3 g

Ingredients

- 1 1/2 C. flour, plus
- 1 tbsp flour
- 1 tbsp salt
- 2 tsps black pepper
- 2 tsps Italian herb seasoning
- 3 lbs boneless skinless chicken breasts
- 3 fluid oz vegetable oil, divided
- 1 lb penne pasta
- 1 tbsp garlic, chopped
- 1 red pepper, julienne cut
- 1/2 C. white wine
- 1/2 lb whole spinach leaves, stemmed
- 12 fluid oz heavy cream
- 1 C. parmesan cheese, grated

Directions

1. Before you do anything set the oven to 350 F.
2. Get a shallow dish: Mix in it 1 1/2 C. flour, salt, black pepper and Italian herb seasoning. Place a large oven proof skillet on medium heat then heat in it some oil.
3. Coat the chicken breasts with the flour mix then brown it in the skillet for 4 min on each side. Transfer the skillet with chicken to the oven and cook it for 17 min.
4. Cook the penne pasta by following the directions on the package until it becomes dente. Drain it and place it aside.
5. To make the sauce:
6. Place a large saucepan on medium heat. Add to it 1 oz of oil. Cook in it the red pepper with garlic for 1 min. Stir in the flour.
7. Stir in the wine and coo them for 1 min. Add the cream and spinach then cook them until they start boiling. Stir in the cheese until it melts.
8. Get a large mixing bowl: Toss the pasta with 1/2 of the sauce. Serve the pasta warm with chicken then drizzle the remaining sauce on top.
9. Enjoy.

CHUNKY Spinach Bean Soup

Prep Time: 10 mins
Total Time: 40 mins

Servings per Recipe: 6
Calories   370.6
Fat   11.3 g
Cholesterol   0 mg
Sodium   725.5 mg
Carbohydrates   50 g
Protein   19.2 g

Ingredients

1/4 C. olive oil
1 medium onion, chopped
4 garlic cloves, minced
2 carrots, chopped
2 stalks celery, chopped
1/4 tsp dried thyme
1 bay leaf
3 (14 oz) cans chicken broth
1 (14 oz) can diced tomatoes, undrained
2 (15 oz) cans white beans, any variety
1 (10 oz) packaged frozen chopped spinach, thawed
3/4 C. macaroni, uncooked
salt and pepper
grated parmesan cheese, and or pecorino romano cheese, to serve

Directions

1. Mash half can of beans.
2. Place a large soup pot on medium heat. Add the oil to it and heat it. Add the onion, garlic, carrots, celery and thyme then cook them for 10 min.
3. Stir in the broth with bay leaf, beans and tomato, spinach, salt and pepper then cook them until they start simmering then simmer the soup for 25 min.
4. Stir in the macaroni and cook the soup for 10 min. Serve the soup warm with some parmesan cheese.
5. Enjoy.

Famous Zuppa Toscana

🍲 Prep Time: 15 mins
🕐 Total Time: 45 mins

Servings per Recipe: 6
Calories   151.7
Fat   2.4 g
Cholesterol   6.8 mg
Sodium   110.5 mg
Carbohydrates   28.7 g
Protein   6.1 g

Ingredients

2 C. spicy beef sausage (Jimmy Dean)
1 medium onion, diced
2 garlic cloves, minced
4 tbsps chicken base
2 quarts water
1/2 tsp dried thyme
1 bay leaf

4 C. coarsely chopped potatoes
6 C. chopped fresh kale
5 oz evaporated milk
parmesan cheese

Directions

1. Place a large skillet on medium heat, add the sausages and cook them for 6 min while breaking them with the spatula. Drain them and set them aside.
2. Slice the ale and set it aside.
3. Place a soup pot on medium heat. Add the oil and heat it. Cook in it the onion with garlic for 4 min.
4. Stir in the water with chicken base, seasonings and potato, kale and cooked sausages. Cook the soup until it starts boiling. Put on the lid and keep the soup simmering for 20 min.
5. Stir in the milk and cook the soup for 4 min. Serve it warm right away.
6. Enjoy.

MUSTARD
Sausage Soup

Prep Time: 15 mins
Total Time: 1 hr 10 mins

Servings per Recipe: 8
Calories	444
Fat	23.7 g
Cholesterol	41.9 mg
Sodium	1373.8 mg
Carbohydrates	38.6 g
Protein	19.1 g

Ingredients

3 (14 oz) cans chicken broth
9 C. water
3 -5 pieces turkey bacon
1 lb Italian sausage, loose-ground
4 large russet potatoes, skin-on and cut into bite sized chunks
1 large white onion, finely chopped
3 garlic cloves, crushed
2 tbsps olive oil
2/3 C. half-and-half

1/2-1 1/2 tsp salt (to taste)
1/2-1 tbsp black pepper (to taste)
1/2-1 tsp ground cayenne pepper
1/2 tsp mustard powder, ground
1/4-1/2 tsp fennel seed, ground (optional)
2 C. kale leaves, chopped (optional)

Directions

1. Place a large skillet on medium heat. Cook in it the bacon strips until they become crisp. Drain the bacon and crumble it then set it aside.
2. Add the onion with olive oil and sausages to the skillet then cook them for 10 min while stirring often.
3. Place a large pot on medium heat. Add the water with broth, potato and salt then bring them to a low boil.
4. Stir in the cooked sausages mix with garlic, powders, and half-and-half. Bring the soup to a simmer then put on the lid and cook it for 30 min.
5. Stir in the kale leaves and turn off the heat. Serve the soup warm
6. Enjoy.

Sunny Hot Spaghetti

Prep Time: 4 mins
Total Time: 16 mins

Servings per Recipe: 2
Calories   627.9
Fat   30.4 g
Cholesterol   0 mg
Sodium   3728.5 mg
Carbohydrates   77.1 g
Protein   14.2 g

Ingredients

- 2 1/2 C. cooked spaghetti
- 1/4 C. olive oil
- 8 pepperoncini peppers, finely minced
- 1/2 C. spaghetti sauce (Muir Glen Garlic Roasted Garlic is by far the best I've found)
- 1 tsp oregano
- 1 tsp garlic granules or 2 tbsps fresh garlic, minced fine

Directions

1. Place a large pan on medium heat. Heat the oil in it. Add the herbs with peppers and cook them for 4 min.
2. Stir in the sauce with cooked spaghetti then cook it for 3 min.
3. Serve your spaghetti warm right away.
4. Enjoy.

CANNELLINI
Sausage Pie

Prep Time: 30 mins
Total Time: 45 mins

Servings per Recipe: 5
Calories   624.5
Fat   29.4 g
Cholesterol   88 mg
Sodium   1286.4 mg
Carbohydrates   54.4 g
Protein   35.3 g

Ingredients

3/4 lb Italian sausage, optional
1 (28 oz) jar spaghetti sauce with mushrooms (we use Prego)
1 (19 oz) can cannellini beans, rinsed and drained
1/2 tsp dried thyme

1 1/2 C. shredded mozzarella cheese
1 (8 oz) package refrigerated crescent dinner rolls

Directions

1. Before you do anything set the oven to 425 F. Grease a large oven proof skillet with oil.
2. Place a large skillet on medium heat. Add the sausages and cook them for 6 min. Drain and discard the grease.
3. Stir in the spaghetti sauce, beans and thyme then cook them for 5 min. Turn off the heat and stir in fold in the mozzarella cheese.
4. Spoon the sausage mix into the skillet then top it with the crescent rolls dough. Cook the pie in the oven for 14 min. Serve your pie warm.
5. Enjoy.

Zesty Chicken Roast

🥣 Prep Time: 10 mins
🕐 Total Time: 55 mins

Servings per Recipe: 2
Calories   172.3
Fat   6.5 g
Cholesterol   75.5 mg
Sodium   137.8 mg
Carbohydrates   1.9 g
Protein   25.4 g

Ingredients

1/2 tbsp olive oil
2 garlic cloves, finely minced
1/2 lemon, zest of
1/2 tbsp lemon juice
2 boneless skinless chicken breasts
fresh ground black pepper
salt

2 tbsps fresh oregano (rosemary, thyme or sage would probably work as well)

Directions

1. Before you do anything set the oven to 375 F. Cover a baking sheet with a piece of parchment paper.
2. Get a small mixing bowl: Mix the oil with garlic, lemon zest and juice. Season the chicken with some salt and pepper then massage the lemon mix into it. Place it in the fridge until ready to cook.
3. Place the chicken on the baking sheet and cook it in the oven for 22 min. Sprinkle the herbs all over the chicken the cook it in the oven for 27 min.
4. Place the chicken aside to rest for 5 min then serve it.
5. Enjoy.

TRADITIONAL
Italian Mussels

Prep Time: 45 mins
Total Time: 1 hr

Servings per Recipe: 2
Calories 383.8
Fat 17.9g
Cholesterol 110.1mg
Sodium 918.5mg
Carbohydrates 14.2g
Protein 34.5g

Ingredients

1 1/4 lbs mussels, cleaned and debearded
2 tbsp butter
1 1/2 tbsp onions, minced
1 garlic clove, minced
1 small tomatoes, chopped
1/4 tsp oregano
salt & freshly ground black pepper (to taste)
1/4 C. dry white wine

Directions

1. In a large bowl of salted water, soak the mussels with flour for about 30 minutes.
2. With a brush, clean the mussels and place in another bowl of clean water.
3. With a paper towel, pat dry the mussels.
4. In a large pan, melt the butter and sauté the onion till tender.
5. Stir in the garlic and sauté for about 1 minute.
6. Stir in the tomato, salt, black pepper and oregano and cook till the tomatoes become tender.
7. Stir in the wine and bring to a boil.
8. Add the mussels and simmer, covered for about 4 minutes.
9. Uncover and stir the mussels and simmer, covered for about 2-4 minutes.
10. Discard any unopened mussels.
11. Serve immediately.

Parmesan Beef Cakes

Prep Time: 20 mins
Total Time: 28 mins

Servings per Recipe: 6
Calories	357.4
Fat	26 g
Cholesterol	96.9 mg
Sodium	541.2 mg
Carbohydrates	1.6 g
Protein	27.8 g

Ingredients

1 1/2 lbs ground beef round
3 garlic cloves, crushed
1/2 tsp salt
1/4 tsp fresh coarse ground black pepper
1 C. grated parmesan cheese
1/3 C. chopped parsley
Other Ingredients:

1 tbsp olive oil
1 tbsp butter
1/3 C. chopped parsley
lemon wedge

Directions

1. Get a large mixing bowl: Add the beef with salt, pepper, cheese, garlic and 1/3 of parsley then mix them well.
2. Shape the beef mix into 1 1/4 inch thick cakes. Place them on a large baking sheet and let them rest for 15 min.
3. Place a large skillet on medium heat. Add the oil with butter to the skillet and cook them until they melts. Cook the beef cakes for 5 min per side.
4. Serve the beef cakes with the remaining parsley.
5. Enjoy.

NUTTY
Vanilla Biscuits

🥣 Prep Time: 15 mins
⏰ Total Time: 55 mins

Servings per Recipe: 1
Calories 45.2
Fat 1.7 g
Cholesterol 9.3 mg
Sodium 12.8 mg
Carbohydrates 6.4 g
Protein 1.4 g

Ingredients

2 C. all-purpose flour
3/4 C. sugar
1 1/2 tsps baking powder
1/2 tsp ground cinnamon
6 oz whole unblanched almonds (about 1 1/2 C.)

3 large eggs
2 tsps vanilla extract

Directions

1. Before you do anything set the oven to 350 F. Line up to baking pans with parchment paper
2. Get a large mixing bowl: Mix the flour, sugar, baking powder, almonds, and cinnamon.
3. Get a mixing bowl: Mix the egg with vanilla.
4. Add the vanilla mix with to the flour mix and whisk them until you get a smooth dough.
5. Place the dough on a working surface and divide it in half then shape each one into a log. Place each log on a baking sheet and flatten them slightly with the palm of your hand.
6. Cook the dough logs in the oven for 38 min. Remove the dough logs from the oven and place them aside to cool down completely.
7. Place the oven racks in the upper and lower thirds.
8. Cut the logs into 1/3 inch thick slices then place lay them on the lined up baking sheet. Cook the biscuits in the oven for 28 min.
9. Allow the biscuits to cool down completely then serve them.
10. Enjoy.

Tomato Cream Dip

Prep Time: 10 mins
Total Time: 50 mins

Servings per Recipe: 6
Calories   244.9
Fat   22.8 g
Cholesterol   62.7 mg
Sodium   148.1 mg
Carbohydrates   6.4 g
Protein   5.3 g

Ingredients

1 garlic clove, pressed
1 C. sour cream
1 (250 g) package cream cheese, room temperature
1 C. fresh basil, chopped
4 medium tomatoes, seeded and chopped

Directions

1. Get a food processor: add the sour cream, cream cheese, garlic and half the basil then process them several times until they become smooth.
2. Get a serving bowl: Spoon the cream mix into the bowl then top it with tomato and basil. Serve the dip right away.
3. Enjoy.

SAUCY Beef Skillet

Prep Time: 5 mins
Total Time: 45 mins

Servings per Recipe: 6
Calories	361.1
Fat	24 g
Cholesterol	58.3 mg
Sodium	578.8 mg
Carbohydrates	18.4 g
Protein	18.3 g

Ingredients

500 g minced beef
4 tbsps olive oil
1 onion, finely diced
2 garlic cloves, peeled and crushed
1 tsp allspice
1 tsp cinnamon
1 tsp paprika

130 g tomato paste
500 g pasta sauce
1 tbsp beef stock, dried instant
2 bay leaves
Worcestershire sauce, dash

Directions

1. Place a large pan on high heat. Heat the oil in it. Add the onion, garlic, beef and spices then cook them for 6 min.
2. Stir in the tomato and pasta sauce, paprika, beef stock, bay leaves, salt and pepper then cook them for 30 min on low heat while stirring often.
3. Serve your saucy beef warm with some pasta.
4. Enjoy.

Sunny Ranch Chicken Soup

Prep Time: 10 mins
Total Time: 30 mins

Servings per Recipe: 4
Calories	421.4
Fat	9.3 g
Cholesterol	75.5 mg
Sodium	916.2 mg
Carbohydrates	42.6 g
Protein	43.3 g

Ingredients

- 1 tbsp olive oil
- 4 boneless skinless chicken breast halves, cut into bite-size pieces
- 2 shallots, minced
- 2 garlic cloves, minced
- 2 (15 oz) cans cannellini beans, rinsed and drained
- 2 (14 oz) cans reduced-chicken broth
- 1 C. baby carrots, cut in half
- 1 C. seeded diced tomato
- 1 (1 oz) packet Hidden Valley Original Ranch DRESSINGMix
- 1 piece parmesan rind
- 1 (10 oz) bag fresh spinach, coarsely chopped
- grated parmesan cheese

Directions

1. Place a large pot on medium heat. Heat the oil in it. Cook in it the chicken, shallots and garlic for 6 min. Add the beans, broth, carrots, tomatoes and seasoning mix then cook them until they start boiling.
2. Turn the heat to low then bring the soup to a simmer and cook it for 15 min. Stir in the spinach and cook the soup for 4 min.
3. Serve the soup and garnish it with some parmesan cheese.
4. Enjoy.

MILANESE Torta

Prep Time: 30 mins
Total Time: 1 hr 37 mins

Servings per Recipe: 6
Calories 483.6
Fat 22.3 g
Cholesterol 154.4 mg
Sodium 798.4 mg
Carbohydrates 42.2 g
Protein 29.9 g

Ingredients

1 1/3 C. Bisquick baking mix
1 (15 -16 oz) can cannellini beans, drained, rinsed, and mashed
1/3 C. Italian DRESSING
1 1/2 C. cooked chicken, diced
1 (10 oz) package frozen chopped spinach, thawed and squeezed to drain
1 C. mozzarella cheese, shredded
3 eggs, slightly beaten
1 1/4 C. milk
1/3 C. slivered almonds, LIGHTLY toasted

Directions

1. Before you do anything set the oven to 375 F. Grease a casserole dish with some butter or oil.
2. Get a small mixing bowl: Whisk the eggs with milk.
3. Get a large mixing bowl: add the baking mix, beans, and DRESSING then combine them completely. Spread the dressing mix in the bottom of the greased casserole.
4. Top it with the chicken, spinach and cheese followed by the eggs mix. Sprinkle the almonds on top then cook the tart in the oven for 1 h.
5. Serve it warm with some ketchup.
6. Enjoy.

Puttanesca (Southern Italian Style)

Prep Time: 25 mins
Total Time: 40 mins

Servings per Recipe: 4
Calories   490 kcal
Fat   34 g
Carbohydrates   38.7g
Protein   9.3 g
Cholesterol   44 mg
Sodium   728 mg

Ingredients

- 8 oz. pasta
- 1/2 C. olive oil
- 3 cloves garlic, minced
- 2 C. diced tomatoes, pushed through a sieve
- 4 anchovy filets, rinsed and diced
- 2 tbsps tomato paste
- 3 tbsps capers
- 20 Greek olives, pitted and coarsely diced
- 1/2 tsp crushed red pepper flakes

Directions

1. Boil your pasta in water and salt for 9 mins then remove all the liquids.
2. Now being to stir fry your garlic in oil until it is browned all over.
3. Then add the tomatoes and cook the mix for 7 mins before adding in: the pepper flakes, anchovies, olives, tomato paste, and capers.
4. Let the mix cook for 12 mins and stir everything at least 2 times.
5. Now add in the pasta and stir everything to evenly coat the noodles.
6. Enjoy.

ITALIAN STYLE
Cod

Prep Time: 10 mins
Total Time: 25 mins

Servings per Recipe: 4
Calories   230 kcal
Fat   9.4 g
Carbohydrates   8.2g
Protein   21.2 g
Cholesterol   41 mg
Sodium   459 mg

Ingredients

2 tbsps olive oil
1 onion, thinly sliced
2 cloves garlic, minced
1 (14.5 oz.) can diced tomatoes
1/2 C. black olives, pitted and sliced

1 tbsp diced fresh parsley
1/2 C. dry white wine
1 lb cod fillets

Directions

1. Stir fry your garlic and onions in olive oil until tender then combine in: wine, tomatoes, parsley, and olives.
2. Let the mix gently boil for 7 mins then add in the cod.
3. Let the cod gently cook for 7 more mins until it is fully done.
4. Enjoy.

Clams Toscano

🥣 Prep Time: 15 mins
🕐 Total Time: 30 mins

Servings per Recipe: 6
Calories 227 kcal
Fat 15.7 g
Carbohydrates 4.4g
Protein 3.2 g
Cholesterol 47 mg
Sodium 126 mg

Ingredients

- 1/2 C. butter
- 5 cloves garlic, minced
- 2 C. dry white wine
- 1 tbsp dried oregano
- 1 tbsp dried parsley
- 1 tsp crushed red pepper flakes (optional)
- 36 clams in shell, scrubbed

Directions

1. Stir fry your garlic in butter for 60 secs then add in the pepper flakes, wine, parsley, and oregano.
2. Stir the mix then add in the clams.
3. Place a lid on the pan and let everything cook until the clams have opened.
4. Divide the mix between serving bowls.
5. Enjoy.

PASTA
Rustic

Prep Time: 10 mins
Total Time: 35 mins

Servings per Recipe: 4
Calories	717 kcal
Carbohydrates	92.8 g
Cholesterol	31 mg
Fat	32.9 g
Protein	18.1 g
Sodium	491 mg

Ingredients

1 lb farfalle (bow tie) pasta
1/3 C. olive oil
1 clove garlic, chopped
1/4 C. butter
2 small zucchini, quartered and sliced
1 onion, chopped
1 tomato, chopped
1 (8 oz) package mushrooms, sliced
1 tbsp dried oregano
1 tbsp paprika
salt and pepper to taste

Directions

1. Boil your pasta for 10 mins in water and salt. Remove excess liquid and set aside.
2. Fry your salt, pepper, garlic, paprika, zucchini, oregano, mushrooms, onion, and tomato, for 17 mins in olive oil.
3. Mix the veggies and pasta.
4. Enjoy.

Simple Sundried Tomato Pasta

Prep Time: 8 hrs
Total Time: 8 hrs 20 mins

Servings per Recipe: 8
Calories   1027 kcal
Carbohydrates   102.5 g
Cholesterol   19 mg
Fat   59.4 g
Protein   24.5 g
Sodium   857 mg

Ingredients

- 2/3 C. chopped fresh basil
- 1 (28 oz) can diced tomatoes
- 1 1/2 tsps diced garlic
- 1 (6 oz) can sliced black olives
- 1 1/2 C. olive oil
- 1 tsp salt
- 1 tsp ground black pepper
- 1/2 C. chopped fresh chives
- 1/2 C. chopped sun-dried tomatoes
- 1 tsp mashed red pepper flakes
- 6 oz goat cheese
- 2 (16 oz) packages farfalle pasta

Directions

1. Get a bowl, mix: pepper flakes, basil, sun dried tomatoes, diced tomatoes, chives, garlic, pepper, olives, salt, and olive oil. Place plastic over the bowl, and set in the fridge for 7 to 12 hours.
2. Before using the mix, let it get to room temp.
3. Boil your pasta in salt and water for 10 mins. Remove the excess liquid, mix pasta with sauce, and goat cheese.
4. Enjoy.

PEPPERONI
Pasta

Prep Time: 20 mins
Total Time: 40 mins

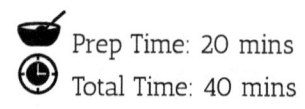

Servings per Recipe: 6
Calories	517 kcal
Carbohydrates	62.3 g
Cholesterol	28 mg
Fat	21.4 g
Protein	18 g
Sodium	782 mg

Ingredients

- 2 tbsps olive oil
- 1 clove garlic, mashed
- 1 onion, diced
- 1 large tomato, cubed
- 1 C. kalamata olives, pitted and chopped
- 1/3 C. sliced pepperoni sausage, cut into strips
- 1/2 C. sliced fresh mushrooms
- 2 tbsps capers
- salt and pepper to taste
- 1 lb pasta
- 1 C. smoked mozzarella cheese, cubed

Directions

1. Boil your pasta for 10 mins in water and salt. Then drain the water. Set aside.
2. Get a frying pan, stir fry: onions, and garlic, in olive oil until onions are see through.
3. Combine in your salt and pepper, tomato, pepperoni, capers, olives, and mushrooms. Bring to a simmer for 3 mins.
4. Finally add your pasta to the sauce. Garnish with mozzarella.
5. Enjoy.

A Light Thai Inspired Pasta

Prep Time: 10 mins
Total Time: 15 mins

Servings per Recipe: 4
Calories   254 kcal
Carbohydrates   43.4 g
Cholesterol   0 mg
Fat   5.9 g
Protein   8.7 g
Sodium   43 mg

Ingredients

- 1 tbsp sesame oil
- 8 oz dry fettuccine pasta
- 1/2 tsp soy sauce
- 2 green onions, chopped
- 3/4 C. fresh bean sprouts
- 1 pinch cayenne pepper
- 1 pinch ground white pepper
- 1 pinch garlic powder
- 1 tbsp toasted sesame seeds

Directions

1. Boil your pasta for 10 mins in salt and water. Drain excess liquid. Set aside.
2. Get a frying pan, stir fry: pasta, soy sauce, garlic powder, green onions, pepper, bean sprouts, black pepper, and cayenne for 5 mins.
3. Garnish with toasted sesame.
4. Enjoy.

BACON
Linguine

🥣 Prep Time: 5 mins
🕐 Total Time: 15 mins

Servings per Recipe: 6
Calories	477 kcal
Carbohydrates	50.1 g
Cholesterol	25 mg
Fat	25 g
Protein	15.2 g
Sodium	345 mg

Ingredients

- 5 shallots, chopped
- 4 cloves garlic, chopped
- 6 oz turkey, diced, optional
- 2 C. fresh sliced mushrooms
- 2 pinches freshly ground black pepper
- 2 pinches dried oregano
- 1/2 C. chicken broth
- 1/4 C. olive oil
- 1 (12 oz) package linguine pasta
- 1/2 C. freshly grated Parmesan cheese

Directions

1. Boil your pasta for 10 mins in salt and water. Remove excess liquid. Set to the side.
2. Get a frying pan and fry your bacon until brown. Then mix in your mushrooms, shallots, and garlic. Cook for another 2 mins. Finally add your broth, oregano, and pepper.
3. Boil everything for 2 mins. Place a lid on the pan. Lower the heat and simmer for 8 mins.
4. Cover your pasta with the broth and some olive oil. Garnish the pasta with some more pancetta, mushrooms, and parmesan.
5. Enjoy.

Easy Mushroom Pasta

Prep Time: 3 mins
Total Time: 15 mins

Servings per Recipe: 5
Calories   526 kcal
Carbohydrates   64.2 g
Cholesterol   106 mg
Fat   22 g
Protein   18.2 g
Sodium   889 mg

Ingredients

- 1 (16 oz) package egg noodles
- 1 (10.75 oz) can condensed cream of mushroom soup
- 1 C. cubed processed cheese
- 2 tbsps butter
- 1/4 C. milk
- 1 tsp garlic powder
- salt and pepper to taste

Directions

1. Boil your pasta in salt and water for 10 mins. Remove excess liquid.
2. Get a pan and heat and stir until cheese melted: salt and pepper, mushroom soup, garlic powder, cheese, milk, and butter.
3. Once your cheese is melted mix in your noodles and heat for 1 more min. Coat evenly.
4. Enjoy.

CAJUN STYLE
Penne

Prep Time: 15 mins
Total Time: 45 mins

Servings per Recipe: 8
Calories 457 kcal
Carbohydrates 68 g
Cholesterol 45 mg
Fat 9.6 g
Protein 24.7 g
Sodium 1107 mg

Ingredients

1 lb penne pasta
2 tbsps butter, divided
4 boneless, skinless chicken breasts, trimmed of fat and cut crosswise into 1/4-inch slices
2 tbsps Cajun-style blackened seasoning
4 cloves garlic, chopped
1 large red onion, cut into wedges
1 green bell pepper, seeded and sliced into strips
1 red bell pepper, seeded and sliced into strips
1 yellow bell pepper, seeded and sliced into strips
1 tsp mashed red pepper flakes
1/4 tsp curry powder
salt and pepper to taste
2 (24 oz) jars meatless spaghetti sauce

Directions

1. Boil pasta in salt and water for 10 mins. Drain excess liquid. Set aside.
2. Get a frying pan and stir fry your chicken in 1 tbsp of butter until fully done and brown. Remove chicken from the pan.
3. Fry onions, salt and pepper, garlic, curry powder, all the julienned peppers, and red pepper flakes until the onions have browned and everything is soft. Mix back in your chicken and the tomato sauce.
4. Heat for 3 mins. Let the flavors settle for 5 mins.
5. Enjoy.

Fresh Seasoning Pasta

Prep Time: 15 mins
Total Time: 30 mins

Servings per Recipe: 4
Calories	379 kcal
Carbohydrates	32.9 g
Cholesterol	102 mg
Fat	24.8 g
Protein	7.1 g
Sodium	216 mg

Ingredients

- 1/2 lb uncooked pasta
- 1/2 C. butter
- 4 cloves garlic, diced
- 3 tbsps chopped fresh basil
- 1 tbsp chopped fresh thyme
- 1 tsp dried marjoram
- 1 tsp ground savory
- 1 tbsp chopped fresh parsley
- salt to taste
- ground black pepper to taste
- 2 tbsps sliced black olives

Directions

1. Boil pasta in salt and water for 10 mins. Remove liquid and set aside.
2. Get a frying pan and melt some butter, and all the seasonings. Cook for 3 mins to flavor your butter.
3. Coat your pasta with the flavored butter. Add some salt and pepper, and garnish with olives.
4. Enjoy.

ALFREDO
Done Right

Prep Time: 20 mins
Total Time: 40 mins

Servings per Recipe: 4
Calories	645 kcal
Carbohydrates	39.7 g
Cholesterol	151 mg
Fat	42.7 g
Protein	28.3 g
Sodium	355 mg

Ingredients

6 oz dry fettuccine pasta
1 (8 oz) package cream cheese
6 tbsps butter
1/2 C. milk
1/2 tsp garlic powder
salt and pepper to taste
2 skinless, boneless chicken breast halves - cooked and cubed
2 C. chopped fresh broccoli
2 small zucchini, julienned
1/2 C. chopped red bell pepper

Directions

1. Boil your pasta in salt and water for 10 mins. Remove excess liquid and set aside.
2. Get a frying pan and mix: milk, garlic powder, cream cheese, salt, pepper, and butter. Heat until cheese is melted and everything is even and smooth. Lightly boil for 4 mins to increase thickness.
3. Add your chicken, red pepper, zucchini, and broccoli and continue simmering for 4 more mins.
4. Toss pasta with alfredo.
5. Enjoy.

Pasta Cajun II

Prep Time: 20 mins
Total Time: 40 mins

Servings per Recipe: 2
Calories	935 kcal
Carbohydrates	54 g
Cholesterol	271 mg
Fat	61.7 g
Protein	43.7 g
Sodium	1189 mg

Ingredients

- 4 oz linguine pasta
- 2 skinless, boneless chicken breast halves
- 2 tsps Cajun seasoning
- 2 tbsps butter
- 1 red bell pepper, sliced
- 1 green bell pepper, sliced
- 4 fresh mushrooms, sliced
- 1 green onion, chopped
- 1 C. heavy cream
- 1/4 tsp dried basil
- 1/4 tsp lemon pepper
- 1/4 tsp salt
- 1/8 tsp garlic powder
- 1/8 tsp ground black pepper
- 1/4 C. grated Parmesan cheese

Directions

1. Boil pasta in salt and water for 10 mins. Remove liquid excess. Set aside.
2. Coat your chicken with Cajun seasoning evenly. Then fry in butter for 8 mins. Continue stir frying the chicken with: green onion, mushrooms, and red and green bell peppers for 4 more mins.
3. Set the heat to low and combine in your garlic powder, cream, lemon pepper, salt, basil, and black pepper. Heat for 3 mins. Then mix in your pasta and heat for another 2 mins.
4. Garnish with some parmesan.
5. Enjoy.

CLAMS, Shrimp, and Snapper Stew

🥣 Prep Time: 10 mins
🕐 Total Time: 1 hr 10 mins

Servings per Recipe: 6
Calories   395 kcal
Fat   7.4 g
Carbohydrates   31.9 g
Protein   48.3 g
Cholesterol   125 mg
Sodium   1006 mg

Ingredients

1 tbsp olive oil
1 onion, diced
3 cloves garlic, finely diced
1 carrot, diced
2 celery ribs, diced
2 bay leaves
1 C. diced fresh parsley
red pepper flakes to taste
1 (28 oz.) can whole peeled tomatoes, mashed
1 1/2 lbs red snapper fillets, cut into 2 inch pieces
1/2 C. white vinegar
salt and ground black pepper to taste
3 C. fish stock
1 lb clams in shell, scrubbed
1/2 lb medium shrimp, with shells
6 (3/4 inch thick) slices Italian bread, toasted

Directions

1. Stir fry the following in olive oil for 7 mins: pepper flakes, onions, parsley, garlic, bay leaves, carrots, celery.
2. Now combine in the mashed tomatoes and continue cooking everything for 20 mins then add: wine, vinegar, and fish.
3. Let the mix continue to cook for 12 mins then add the stock, set the heat to low, place a lid on the pot, and continue cooking everything for 12 more mins.
4. Now slowly add in the clams.
5. Let the clams cook for 4 mins until they open then add the shrimp and cook them for 4 more mins as well.
6. To serve the dish add a piece of bread to the bottom of a serving bowl and top the bread with the tomato mix.
7. Enjoy.

Meatballs
Done Right

🥣 Prep Time: 1 hr 15 mins
🕐 Total Time: 8 hrs 15 mins

Servings per Recipe: 8
Calories   841 kcal
Fat   45.1 g
Carbohydrates   65.6g
Protein   40.3 g
Cholesterol   134 mg
Sodium   2164 mg

Ingredients

- 3 lbs lean ground beef
- 5 tbsps ground oregano
- 5 tbsps dried parsley, crushed
- 1 clove garlic, diced
- 1 (1 oz.) package dry onion soup mix
- 2 C. Italian-style dry bread crumbs
- 3 (28 oz.) jars spaghetti sauce

Directions

1. Coat a jelly roll pan with oil then set your oven to 350 degrees before doing anything else.
2. Get a bowl, combine: garlic, beef, parsley, and oregano.
3. Stir the mix then add in the bread crumbs and the onion soup mix.
4. Combine everything evenly then use a 1 oz. scoop to form meatballs from the mix.
5. Place the meatballs in the dish and cook them for 65 mins in the oven.
6. Once the meatballs are done cooking get your pasta sauce and meatballs boiling in a saucepan.
7. Once the mix is boiling set the heat to low and let everything gently cook for 5 hrs.
8. Enjoy.

EASY
Biscotti

Prep Time: 25 mins
Total Time: 1 hr 35 mins

Servings per Recipe: 30
Calories	138 kcal
Fat	7.8 g
Carbohydrates	15.5g
Protein	2.2 g
Cholesterol	25 mg
Sodium	89 mg

Ingredients

3/4 C. butter
1 C. white sugar
2 eggs
1 1/2 tsps vanilla extract
2 1/2 C. all-purpose flour
1 tsp ground cinnamon

3/4 tsp baking powder
1/2 tsp salt
1 C. hazelnuts

Directions

1. Coat a baking dish with oil then set your oven to 350 degrees before doing anything else.
2. Get a bowl, combine: sugar and butter. Mix the contents until it is creamy.
3. Now add in the vanilla and the eggs. Stir the mix then sift in: salt, flour, baking powder, and cinnamon. Stir everything again then add in the hazelnuts.
4. Now form your dough into 2 foot long cylinders.
5. Lay the cylinders on the cookie sheet and flatten them.
6. Let the dough cook in the oven for 35 mins. Then let the loaves lose their heat.
7. Now cut each one diagonally and place everything back in the oven for 12 more mins.
8. Flip the loaves after 6 mins of cooking.
9. Enjoy.

Italian Tuscan Soup

Prep Time: 15 mins
Total Time: 1 hr 10 mins

Servings per Recipe: 6
Calories	459 kcal
Fat	34.1 g
Carbohydrates	21.1g
Protein	17.2 g
Cholesterol	87 mg
Sodium	1925 mg

Ingredients

- 1 (16 oz.) package smoked sausage
- 2 potatoes, cut into 1/4-inch slices
- 3/4 C. diced onion
- 6 slices turkey bacon
- 1 1/2 tsps minced garlic
- 2 C. kale - washed, dried, and shredded
- 2 tbsps chicken bouillon powder
- 1 quart water
- 1/3 C. heavy whipping cream

Directions

1. Set your oven to 300 degrees before doing anything else.
2. Place your pieces of sausage on a cookie sheet and cook everything in the oven for 30 mins.
3. Then divide the meat in half and then cut them in half again diagonally.
4. Begin to stir fry your bacon and onions until the onions are translucent then remove the bacon from the pan.
5. Add in the garlic and cook everything for 2 more mins then add the chicken base, potatoes, and water.
6. Let the mix gently boil for 20 mins then add in: the cream, bacon, kale, and sausage.
7. Let the soup cook for 5 mins.
8. Enjoy.

CHICKEN
Marsala Classico

Prep Time: 10 mins
Total Time: 30 mins

Servings per Recipe: 4
Calories	448 kcal
Fat	26.6 g
Carbohydrates	13.3g
Protein	28.8 g
Cholesterol	99 mg
Sodium	543 mg

Ingredients

1/4 C. all-purpose flour for coating
1/2 tsp salt
1/4 tsp ground black pepper
1/2 tsp dried oregano
4 skinless, boneless chicken breast halves – flattened to 1/4 inch thick
4 tbsps butter
4 tbsps olive oil
1 C. sliced mushrooms
1/2 C. Marsala wine
1/4 C. cooking sherry

Directions

1. Get a bowl, combine: oregano, flour, pepper, and salt.
2. Dredge your pieces of chicken in the mix then begin to stir fry the chicken in butter.
3. Let the chicken fry until it is browned all over then add in: the sherry, mushrooms, and wine.
4. Place a lid on the pan and let the contents gently boil for 12 mins.
5. Enjoy.

Maggie's Easy Bruschetta

Prep Time: 15 mins
Total Time: 35 mins

Servings per Recipe: 12
Calories   215 kcal
Fat   8.9 g
Carbohydrates   24.8g
Protein   9.6 g
Cholesterol   12 mg
Sodium   426 mg

Ingredients

- 6 roma (plum) tomatoes, diced
- 1/2 C. sun-dried tomatoes, packed in oil
- 3 cloves minced garlic
- 1/4 C. olive oil
- 2 tbsps balsamic vinegar
- 1/4 C. fresh basil, stems removed
- 1/4 tsp salt
- 1/4 tsp ground black pepper
- 1 French baguette
- 2 C. shredded mozzarella cheese

Directions

1. Get your oven's broiler hot before doing anything else.
2. Now grab a bowl, mix: pepper, roma tomatoes, salt, sun-dried tomatoes, basil, garlic, vinegar, and olive oil.
3. Let this mix sit for 12 mins and begin to slice your bread into 3/4 of inch pieces.
4. Place the pieces of bread on a cookie sheet then place everything under the broiler for 3 mins.
5. Now evenly top each piece of bread with the roma tomato mix.
6. Then add a piece of cheese on top of each one.
7. Cook the bread slices under the broiler for 6 more mins.
8. Enjoy.

AUTHENTIC Eggplant Parmesan

Prep Time: 25 mins
Total Time: 1 hr

Servings per Recipe: 10
Calories	487 kcal
Fat	16 g
Carbohydrates	62.1g
Protein	24.2 g
Cholesterol	73 mg
Sodium	1663 mg

Ingredients

3 eggplant, peeled and thinly sliced
2 eggs, beaten
4 C. Italian seasoned bread crumbs
6 C. spaghetti sauce, divided
1 (16 oz.) package mozzarella cheese, shredded and divided
1/2 C. grated Parmesan cheese, divided
1/2 tsp dried basil

Directions

1. Set your oven to 350 degrees before doing anything else.
2. Coat your pieces of eggplant with egg then with bread crumbs.
3. Now lay the veggies on a cookie sheet and cook them in the oven for 6 mins. Flip the eggplants and cook them for 6 more mins.
4. Coat the bottom of a casserole dish with pasta sauce then layer some of your eggplants in the dish.
5. Top the veggies with some parmesan and mozzarella then layer your eggplants, sauce, and cheese.
6. Continue this pattern until all the ingredients have been used up.
7. Finally coat the layer with some basil and cook everything in the oven for 40 mins.
8. Enjoy.

Roman Fun Pasta

Prep Time: 15 mins
Total Time: 45 mins

Servings per Recipe: 6
Calories   656 kcal
Fat   42.1 g
Carbohydrates   50.9 g
Protein   20.1 g
Cholesterol   111 mg
Sodium   1088 mg

Ingredients

1 (12 oz.) package bow tie pasta
2 tbsps olive oil
1 lb sweet Italian sausage, casings removed and crumbled
1/2 tsp red pepper flakes
1/2 C. diced onion
3 cloves garlic, minced
1 (28 oz.) can Italian-style plum tomatoes, drained and coarsely diced
1 1/2 C. heavy cream
1/2 tsp salt
3 tbsps minced fresh parsley

Directions

1. Boil your pasta in water and salt for 9 mins then remove the liquids.
2. Begin to stir fry your pepper flakes and sausage in oil until it the meat is browned then add the garlic and onions.
3. Let the onions cook until they are soft then add in the salt, cream, and tomatoes.
4. Stir the mix then get everything gently boiling.
5. Let the mix gently cook with a low level of heat for 9 mins then add in the pasta.
6. Stir the mix, to evenly cook the noodles, then coat everything with parsley.
7. Enjoy.

ZUCCHINI
and Spinach Soup

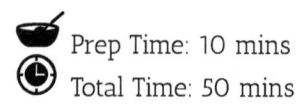

Prep Time: 10 mins
Total Time: 50 mins

Servings per Recipe: 6
Calories 385 kcal
Fat 24.4 g
Carbohydrates 22.5g
Protein 18.8 g
Cholesterol 58 mg
Sodium 1259 mg

Ingredients

1 lb Italian sausage
1 clove garlic, minced
2 (14 oz.) cans beef broth
1 (14.5 oz.) can Italian-style stewed tomatoes
1 C. sliced carrots
1 (14.5 oz.) can great Northern beans, undrained
2 small zucchini, cubed
2 C. spinach - packed, rinsed and torn
1/4 tsp ground black pepper
1/4 tsp salt

Directions

1. Stir fry your garlic and sausage, in a large pot, for 2 mins then combine in the pepper, broth, salt, tomato, and carrots.
2. Stir the mix, place a lid on the pot, and let everything gently boil for 20 mins with a medium to low level of heat.
3. Now add in the zucchini and beans with their sauce.
4. Place the lid back on the pot and continue cooking everything for 17 more mins.
5. Now shut the heat, stir in the spinach, and place the lid back on the pot.
6. Let the spinach wilt for 7 mins then serve the soup.
7. Enjoy.

Classical Risotto

Prep Time: 20 mins
Total Time: 50 mins

Servings per Recipe: 6
Calories	431 kcal
Fat	16.6 g
Carbohydrates	56.6 g
Protein	11.3 g
Cholesterol	29 mg
Sodium	1131 mg

Ingredients

- 6 C. chicken broth, divided
- 3 tbsps olive oil, divided
- 1 lb portobello mushrooms, thinly sliced
- 1 lb white mushrooms, thinly sliced
- 2 shallots, diced
- 1 1/2 C. Arborio rice
- 1/2 C. dry white wine
- sea salt to taste
- freshly ground black pepper to taste
- 3 tbsps finely diced chives
- 4 tbsps butter
- 1/3 C. freshly grated Parmesan cheese

Directions

1. Get your broth warm with a low level of heat. Then begin to stir fry your mushrooms in 2 tbsp of olive oil for 4 mins.
2. Now remove everything from the pot and add in 1 more tbsp of olive oil and begin to fry your shallots in it for 2 mins then add in the rice and stir fry it for 3 mins.
3. Pour in the wine while continuing to stir, and keep stirring, until it is absorbed.
4. Once the wine has been absorbed combine in half a C. of broth and keep stirring until it is absorbed as well.
5. Now for about 20 mins keep pouring in half a C. of broth and stirring the mix until the broth is absorbed by the rice.
6. After 20 mins of forming the risotto, shut the heat and combine in: the parmesan, pepper, mushrooms and their juice, chives, salt, and butter.
7. Enjoy.

TORTELLINI
Classico

Prep Time: 20 mins
Total Time: 1 hr 35 mins

Servings per Recipe: 8
Calories	324 kcal
Fat	20.2 g
Carbohydrates	19.1g
Protein	14.6 g
Cholesterol	50 mg
Sodium	1145 mg

Ingredients

- 1 lb sweet Italian sausage, casings removed
- 1 C. diced onion
- 2 cloves garlic, minced
- 5 C. beef broth
- 1/2 C. water
- 1/2 C. red wine
- 4 large tomatoes - peeled, seeded and diced
- 1 C. thinly sliced carrots
- 1/2 tbsp packed fresh basil leaves
- 1/2 tsp dried oregano
- 1 (8 oz.) can tomato sauce
- 1 1/2 C. sliced zucchini
- 8 oz. fresh tortellini pasta
- 3 tbsps diced fresh parsley

Directions

1. In a large pot brown your sausage all over.
2. Then remove the meat from the pan.
3. Begin to stir fry your garlic and onions in the drippings then add in: the sausage, broth, tomato sauce, water, oregano, wine, basil, tomatoes, and carrots.
4. Get the mix boiling, set the heat to low, and let everything cook for 35 mins.
5. Remove any fat which rises to the top then add in the parsley and zucchini.
6. Continue cooking the mix for 20 more mins before adding in the pasta and letting everything cooking 15 more mins.
7. When serving the dish top it with parmesan.
8. Enjoy.

Feta Fettucine

Prep Time: 15 mins
Total Time: 25 mins

Servings per Recipe:	4
Calories	663 kcal
Fat	39.4 g
Carbohydrates	64.8g
Protein	16.5 g
Cholesterol	11 mg
Sodium	248 mg

Ingredients

- 1 bunch diced fresh cilantro
- 6 tbsps pine nuts
- 1 tsp lemon juice, or to taste
- 1/3 C. crumbled feta cheese
- salt and ground black pepper to taste
- 1/2 C. olive oil
- 1 (12 oz.) package fettucine pasta
- 1 tsp extra-virgin olive oil

Directions

1. Pulse the following in a food processor until minced: black pepper, cilantro, salt, pine nuts, feta cheese, and lemon juice.
2. Now slowly add in half a C. of olive oil while continually running the processor.
3. Boil your pasta for 9 mins in water and salt then remove the liquids.
4. Place the pasta in a bowl and top it with the cilantro sauce.
5. Toss the mix then add some olive oil and toss everything again.
6. Enjoy.

AUTHENTIC
Meatball Sub

Prep Time: 15 mins
Total Time: 1 hr 40 mins

Servings per Recipe: 6
Calories	491 kcal
Fat	21.4 g
Carbohydrates	43.1g
Protein	29.3 g
Cholesterol	75 mg
Sodium	1068 mg

Ingredients

1 1/2 lbs lean ground beef
1/3 C. Italian seasoned bread crumbs
1/2 small onion, diced
1 tsp salt
1/2 C. shredded mozzarella cheese, divided
1 tbsp cracked black pepper
1 tsp garlic powder
1/2 C. marinara sauce
3 hoagie rolls, split lengthwise

Directions

1. Set your oven to 350 degrees before doing anything else.
2. Get a bowl, combine: 1/2 of the mozzarella, beef, garlic powder, bread crumbs, pepper, onions, and salt.
3. Shape the mix into a large loaf then place it in a casserole dish.
4. Cook the meat in the oven for 55 mins then let it cool for 10 mins.
5. Cut the meat into slices then layer the pieces of meat on a roll.
6. Top everything with the marinara then add a topping of cheese.
7. Cover the sandwich with some foil and put everything in the oven for 20 more mins.
8. Let the sandwich cool for 20 mins then cut each one in half.
9. Enjoy.

Capers and Tilapia

Prep Time: 15 mins
Total Time: 25 mins

Servings per Recipe: 4
Calories	262 kcal
Fat	14.2 g
Carbohydrates	5g
Protein	24.2 g
Cholesterol	57 mg
Sodium	222 mg

Ingredients

- 2 tbsps extra virgin olive oil
- 2 tbsps butter
- 1 tbsp minced garlic
- 1 lb tilapia fillets
- salt and ground black pepper to taste
- 1/2 C. sliced fresh button mushrooms
- 2 tbsps drained capers
- 1/2 C. white wine
- 1 lemon, juiced

Directions

1. Stir fry your garlic in butter and olive oil then add the pieces of fish to pan.
2. Top the fish with pepper and salt and fry everything for 3 mins. Flip the fish then coat the opposite side with pepper and salt as well and fry it for 3 mins.
3. Now combine in the wine, capers, and mushrooms.
4. Place a lid on the pot, set the heat to low, and simmer the mix for 8 mins.
5. Take off the lid, add in the lemon juice, and continue cooking everything for 2 more mins.
6. Enjoy.

SOUTHERN
Italian Chicken

🥣 Prep Time: 15 mins
🕘 Total Time: 9 hrs 15 mins

Servings per Recipe: 6
Calories	402 kcal
Fat	22.4 g
Carbohydrates	16.5g
Protein	31.2 g
Cholesterol	97 mg
Sodium	308 mg

Ingredients

- 3 cloves garlic, minced
- 1/3 C. pitted prunes, halved
- 8 small green olives
- 2 tbsps capers, with liquid
- 2 tbsps olive oil
- 2 tbsps red wine vinegar
- 2 bay leaves
- 1 tbsp dried oregano
- salt and pepper to taste
- 1 (3 lb) whole chicken, skin removed and cut into pieces
- 1/4 C. packed brown sugar
- 1/4 C. dry white wine
- 1 tbsp diced fresh parsley, for garnish

Directions

1. Get a bowl, combine: pepper, garlic, salt, prunes, oregano, olives, bay leaves, capers, vinegar, and olive oil.
2. Layer this mix in the bottom of casserole dish then layer the chicken on top. Stir everything then place a covering of plastic around the dish.
3. Put everything in the fridge for 8 hrs.
4. Now set your oven to 350 degrees before doing anything else.
5. Once the oven is hot pour the wine and the brown sugar around the chicken and begin to cook everything in the oven for 65 mins.
6. Baste the meat with the surrounding sauce at least 5 times.
7. When serving the dish top everything with the sauce and drippings and also some fresh parsley.
8. Enjoy.

Roast Beef Sandwiches

Prep Time: 10 mins
Total Time: 6 hrs 10 mins

Servings per Recipe: 6
Calories   557 kcal
Fat   28.8 g
Carbohydrates   38.4g
Protein   31.9 g
Cholesterol   103 mg
Sodium   4233 mg

Ingredients

3 lbs beef chuck roast
3 (1 oz.) packages dry Italian salad dressing mix
1 C. water
1 (16 oz.) jar pepperoncini peppers

8 hamburger buns, split

Directions

1. Place your chuck in the crock of a slow cooker and top the meat with the dressing mix.
2. Now add the water and place a lid on the slow cooker.
3. Cook the meat for 6 hrs with a high level of heat.
4. At the fifth hour remove the meat and shred it into pieces.
5. The meat should easily shred if not add it back to the crock pot.
6. After shredding the meat combine in the peppers and some of the juice.
7. Enjoy with the buns.

TORTELLINI

Prep Time: 20 mins
Total Time: 40 mins

Servings per Recipe: 6
Calories	400 kcal
Fat	19.7 g
Carbohydrates	43.9 g
Protein	14.8 g
Cholesterol	79 mg
Sodium	885 mg

Ingredients

1 (16 oz.) package cheese tortellini
1 (14.5 oz.) can diced tomatoes with garlic and onion
1 C. diced fresh spinach
1/2 tsp salt
1/4 tsp pepper
1 1/2 tsps dried basil
1 tsp minced garlic

2 tbsps all-purpose flour
3/4 C. milk
3/4 C. heavy cream
1/4 C. grated Parmesan cheese

Directions

1. Boil your pasta in water and salt for 9 mins then remove the liquids.
2. At the same time heat and stir the following in a large pot: garlic, tomatoes, basil, spinach, pepper and salt.
3. Once the mix begins to simmer add in a mix of cream, milk, and flour.
4. Stir the mix until everything is smooth then add the parmesan and set the heat to low.
5. Let the mix gently boil for 4 mins then add in your pasta to the sauce after it has cooked.
6. Stir everything.
7. Enjoy.

Italian Baked Turkey-Loaf

Prep Time: 10 mins
Total Time: 1 hr 15 mins

Servings per Recipe: 6
Calories   163 kcal
Fat   7 g
Carbohydrates   8.1g
Protein   17.8 g
Cholesterol   87 mg
Sodium   651 mg

Ingredients

cooking spray
1 lb ground turkey
1 egg
1/4 C. Italian seasoned bread crumbs
1 tsp Italian seasoning
1/2 clove garlic, minced
1/2 tsp ground black pepper, or to taste
1/4 tsp salt, or to taste
2 C. tomato sauce, divided

Directions

1. Coat a casserole dish with nonstick spray then set your oven to 400 degrees before doing anything else.
2. Get a bowl, combine: salt, turkey, black pepper, egg, garlic, bread crumbs, and Italian seasoning.
3. Form the mix into a loaf and place it in the casserole dish.
4. Cook the loaf in the oven for 45 mins then top with 1/2 of the tomato sauce.
5. Let the loaf keep cooking for 12 more mins until it is fully done.
6. Then leave the meat to sit for 15 mins.
7. As the loaf cools get the rest of the tomato sauce hot.
8. When serving your loaf top it liberally with the tomato sauce.
9. Enjoy.

RESTAURANT STYLE
Primavera

Prep Time: 20 mins
Total Time: 50 mins

Servings per Recipe: 8
Calories   477 kcal
Fat   21.8 g
Carbohydrates   50.1g
Protein   20.5 g
Cholesterol   38 mg
Sodium   621 mg

Ingredients

1 (16 oz.) package uncooked farfalle pasta
1 lb hot Italian turkey sausage, cut into 1/2 inch slices
1/2 C. olive oil, divided
4 cloves garlic, diced
1/2 onion, diced
2 small zucchini, diced
2 small yellow squash, diced
6 roma (plum) tomatoes, diced
1 green bell pepper, diced
20 leaves fresh basil
2 tsps chicken bouillon granules
1/2 tsp red pepper flakes
1/2 C. grated Parmesan cheese

Directions

1. Cook your pasta in water and salt for 9 mins then remove all the liquids.
2. Stir fry your sausage until fully done then remove it from the pan.
3. Now begin to stir fry your onions and garlic until the mix is hot then add in: basil, zucchini, bell peppers, squash, and tomatoes.
4. Stir the mix then add in the bouillon and evenly mix it in.
5. Once the bouillon has been added.
6. Combine in the red pepper and the rest of the oil.
7. Keep cooking the mix for 12 more mins then stir in the cheese, sausage, and pasta.
8. Let everything get hot for 7 mins.
9. Enjoy.

ENJOY THE RECIPES?

KEEP ON COOKING WITH 6 MORE FREE COOKBOOKS!

Visit our website and simply enter your email address to join the club and receive your 6 cookbooks.

http://booksumo.com/magnet

https://www.instagram.com/booksumopress/

https://www.facebook.com/booksumo/

CPSIA information can be obtained
at www.ICGtesting.com
Printed in the USA
LVHW100713180520
655899LV00010B/1314